Twenty to **Craft**

Tassels

Carolyn Schulz

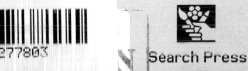

Search Press

Dedication

I'd like to dedicate this book to my dear friend Vivian Peritts. Her enormous contribution was very much appreciated. She was an inspiration but best of all, she made this project a lot of fun!

First published in 2019

Search Press Limited
Wellwood, North Farm Road,
Tunbridge Wells, Kent TN2 3DR

Text copyright © Carolyn Schulz 2019

Photographs by Stacy Grant

Photographs and design copyright
© Search Press Ltd. 2019

ISBN: 978-1-78221-670-4

Publisher's Note

The Publishers and author can accept no responsibility for any consequences arising from the information, advice or instructions given in this publication.

Readers are permitted to reproduce any of the items in this book for their personal use, or for the purposes of selling for charity, free of charge and without the prior permission of the Publishers. Any use of the items for commercial purposes is not permitted without the prior permission of the Publishers.

Suppliers

If you have difficulty in obtaining any of the materials and equipment mentioned in this book, then please visit the Search Press website for details of suppliers:
www.searchpress.com

Visit the Twenty to Make website:
www.20toMake.com

Printed in China through Asia Pacific Offset.

Contents

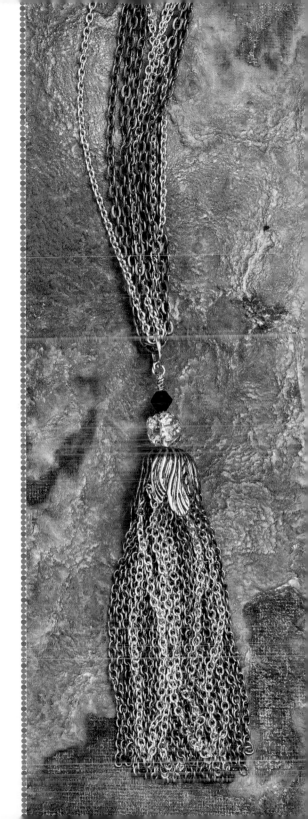

Introduction

I fell in love with tassels when working on the second book in my Jewelry School series, *Bead Stringing*. I was delighted with how a tassel could add sophisticated elegance to a necklace, so I was thrilled to have the opportunity to explore the many different techniques for making tassels, as well as the variety of ways in which they can be used – they make fabulous embellishments for jewellery and fashion and add a special flair to home decor.

It appears that the earliest recorded use of tassels is found in the Bible during the time of Moses and the exodus of the Israelites from Egypt, where tassels were placed on the corners of garments as a sign of holiness. The modern tassel as we know it in the West today is traced back to sixteenth-century France, where *passementiers* served a seven-year apprenticeship to become a master within their guild.

Tassels worn on headwear were used as talismans in the Middle East, while, in the past, Oxford and Cambridge university undergraduates wore them on their caps, black for the ordinary commoner and gold for a gentleman commoner. Tassels on mortarboards continue to be an integral part of the graduation ceremony in high schools and universities in the United States.

Making tassels is easier than you may think. In this book, we will explore a number of techniques using materials and tools that are readily available: many of which you may already have. While tassels alone add something extra to any project, they can also be decorated with other components such as beads or wire, and can be used alongside other embellishments such as pompoms or bows.

Why not have a go at making a tassel for a stunning pair of earrings, or as a fringe to add a unique personal touch to a lampshade? I have almost forty designs that I can't wait to share with you, to inspire your own creations. If you are anything like me, you will be making and adding tassels to your clothes and accessories for years to come!

Tassels: top tips

General notes and advice

• Most of the measurements in this book are approximate as there are several variables, such as how tight or loose you may wrap the threads or cords, or the thickness of the threads themselves.

• When wrapping threads or cords around a cardboard square or a fork (to make a pompom), don't pull them too tight. The cardboard may buckle, and it will be harder for you to slip the threads or cords off the card or fork.

• When wrapping threads or cords around a cardboard square, layer wraps on top of one another. I usually wrap five to eight wraps side by side, then add the remaining wraps over the top of the base layer.

• After trimming the fringe of the tassel (threads, cords and chain), you may find that you need to trim it again after it settles.

Typical tassel

The diagram below shows the various elements of a typical, basic tassel.

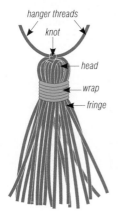

hanger threads
knot
head
wrap
fringe

Wrapping a tassel

The diagram below shows where the wrap begins, to divide the head from the fringe of the basic tassel.

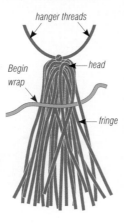

hanger threads
head
Begin wrap
fringe

Making a rolled tassel

(See pages 36–37, *Santa Fe necklace*.)

1 Mark a piece of suede leather with a line, about 1cm (½in) from the top.

2 Cut twelve to fourteen strips up to the 1cm (½in) mark.

3 Fold a length of leather cord in half and glue it to the left edge of the tassel head with clear drying adhesive.

4 Spread the tassel head generously with adhesive and tightly roll the suede head around the leather cord to complete the rolled tassel.

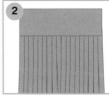

Making a hidden wrap

A hidden wrap is an alternative to knotting the wraps that form the head of the tassel. It leaves a seamless finish and should be started a bit lower on the tassel than when making a knotted wrap (see Wrapping a tassel, opposite).

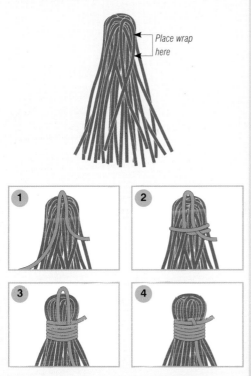

Place wrap here

1 Fold one end of the wrapping thread with about a 5cm (2in) tail. Place the fold against the tassel, just slightly above where you want the wraps to finish. page 33

2 Take the long end of the wrapping thread, pass over the short end of the thread and start wrapping it round.

3 When you have reached the desired number of wraps, slip the long wrapping thread through the fold made in step 1.

4 Gently but firmly pull the short end of the wrapping thread until the long end of the wrapping thread is about halfway behind the wraps made in step 2. Cut off any excess threads.

The following tips and techniques relate to those projects that include jewellery-making.

Making a wrapped loop

1 Hold the wire with a pair of round-nosed pliers – hold the pliers themselves horizontally.

2 Bend the wire at right angles with your finger.

3 Shift the barrels of the round-nosed pliers so they are vertical.

4 Use your fingers to pull the wire tight around the top barrel of the pliers and then down. Pull so that the wire is tight around the barrel and down as far as it can go.

5 Shift the barrels again to make them horizontal. Use your fingers to pull the wire around the barrel of the pliers to form a complete loop.

6 Change to bent-nosed pliers and hold the loop. Twist the wire two or three times, or as many as required, around the gap between the bead and the loop.

7 Use flush cutters to trim the end of the wire.

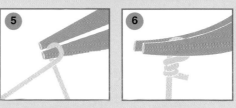

Making a flat coil

1 With round-nose pliers, make a small, tight loop at one end of the wire.

2 Hold the loop formed in step 1 with flat-nose pliers using your dominant hand, and use your non-dominant hand to wrap the remaining wire around the loop. Continue to wrap the wire until the coil reaches your desired size.

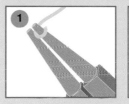
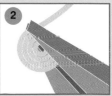

A Hint of Red necklace

Materials:

1 skein of red embroidery floss

8 x 8cm (3 x 3in) cardboard square

60 jet 6 x 4cm (2¼ x 1½in) faceted glass rondelle beads

2 jet 6mm glass bicone beads

10 ruby 6mm glass bicone beads

12 ruby 4mm glass bicone beads

42 silver coloured round metal beads

3 silver coloured 6mm jump rings

2 silver coloured calottes (bead tips)

4 silver coloured 2mm crimp beads

1 silver coloured toggle clasp

30cm (12in) silver coloured beading wire

Clear nail varnish or clear drying adhesive (E6000)

Tools:

Scissors

Chain-nose pliers

Round-nose pliers

Wire cutters

Note

These materials and instructions make two tassels. Set one aside to make a matching embellishment for a clutch bag (see opposite).

Instructions:

1 Cut a 70cm (27½in) length of thread from a skein of embroidery floss, keeping the rest of the skein intact. Cut the thread into four lengths: two 10cm (4in) long and two 25cm (9¾in) long. Set all aside.

2 Fold the remaining skein in half with the two folded ends together. Cut the newly created fold to make two tassels of equal size.

3 Take one tassel (cut in step 2): tie one 5cm (2in) strand of thread (from step 1) into a tight reef knot (square knot), in the middle of the fold. This will form the hanger at the top of the tassel.

4 Hold the tassel 1cm (½in) from the knot in the fold. Take a 25cm (9¾in) length of thread (from step 1). With approximately 1.5cm (½in) hanging below the cut end of the tassel (the fringe), run the thread up to where you are holding the tassel. Wrap the thread around the tassel two or three times, creating a head. Tie a tight reef knot and pull the tails down to the cut end of the tassel.

5 Trim the tails from the knotted tie (from step 4) and trim any other thread ends that extend below the fringe.

6 Use nail varnish or adhesive to seal the knot formed by the hanger threads at the top of the tassel. Cut the threads close to the knot.

7 Open one jump ring with chain-nose pliers and slip it through the hanger strand of thread at the top of the head of the tassel. Close the jump ring.

8 Thread a crimp bead onto one end of the beading wire. With chain-nose pliers, flatten the crimp bead approximately 0.5cm (¼in) from the end of the thread. Repeat with a second crimp bead directly above the first, 3mm (⅛in) from the end.

9 Thread the end of the beading wire (opposite the flattened crimps), passing from the inside to the outside of the calotte cup. Pull the crimps down into the cup of the calotte and with chain-nose pliers, gently close the two sides of the calotte over the crimps. With round-nose pliers, close the hook of the calotte to form a loop.

10 Thread beads onto the beading wire in the following sequence five times: silver metal bead; 4mm ruby bicone bead; silver metal bead; three jet rondelle beads; silver metal bead; 6mm ruby bicone bead; silver metal bead and three jet rondelle beads.

11 Continue with: silver metal bead; 4mm ruby bicone bead; 6mm jet bicone bead; jump ring with the tassel attached; 6mm jet bicone bead and 4mm ruby bicone bead.

12 Create the other side of the necklace by repeating the following sequence five times: silver metal bead; three jet rondelle beads; silver metal bead; 6mm ruby bicone bead; silver metal bead; three jet rondelle beads; silver metal bead and 4mm ruby bicone bead.

13 Finish the beading with: silver metal bead; 4mm ruby bicone bead and silver metal bead.

14 Thread the beading wire through a calotte from the outside to the inside of the cup. Thread on two crimp beads. With chain-nose pliers, push the first crimp bead down deep into the cup of the calotte, at the same time pushing beads below together. Flatten the crimp bead so the beads are close together but not so close that the necklace is stiff. Repeat with a second crimp bead. With wire cutters, trim excess wire. With chain-nose pliers, gently close the two sides of the calotte over the crimps. With round-nose pliers, close the hook of the calotte to form a loop.

15 With chain nose pliers, open a jump ring and attach one side of the clasp to the calotte loop at one end of the necklace. Repeat by attaching the other side of the clasp with the remaining jump ring to the other end of the necklace.

The tassel for this clutch bag clasp has been made in the same way as for the necklace.

Sunburst brooch

Materials:

2 skeins each of three coordinating colours of embroidery floss

Wire brooch pin base, 8cm (3¼in) long

Clear nail varnish or clear drying adhesive (E6000)

Tools:

Four-pronged fork

Scissors

Instructions:

1 Cut two lengths of thread, one 10cm (4in) long and one 20cm (7¾in) long. Set aside.

2 From the skein, wrap thread firmly but not too tightly fifteen times around all four prongs of a fork – hold the fork horizontally to do so. Start with one end of the thread extending 1cm (½in) below the lowest prong of the fork. Finish with the tail of the last wrap extending 1cm (½in) below the lowest prong of the fork.

3 Slip the 10cm (4in) length of thread (from step 1) under the wraps at one side of the fork and slide it up and under the fold at the top of the upper prong of the fork. Tie a tight reef knot (square knot). This is the 'hanger thread'.

4 Slide the wraps of thread from the fork. Hold the tassel with the non-dominant hand between thumb and forefinger approximately 0.5cm (¼in) from the knot in the fold (from step 3). Take the 20cm (7in) length of thread (from step 1). With 1–2cm (½–¾in) hanging below the cut end of the tassel, run the thread up to where the tassel is being held – 0.5cm (¼in) from the knot at the top of tassel. Wrap the thread around the tassel three or four times, creating a head. Tie a tight reef knot and pull down the tails of the knot.

5 Cut the folded threads at the bottom of the tassel (the opposite end of the tassel head) to form the fringe. Trim the tails of the knotted tie from step 4 and the fringe, to create the desired length of the tassel.

6 Make six mini tassels of each colour.

7 Referring to the photograph opposite, tie the tassels to the wire brooch using a reef knot (square knot). Seal the knots with clear nail varnish or drying adhesive and trim the knot tails, leaving a little fringe above the knot.

Use the same coloured threads and mini tassels to create matching sunburst earrings.

Springtime necklace

Materials:

Skeins of embroidery floss:
 1–2 each of pale pink, fuchsia, purple, teal, aqua and pale green, and 2–3 white (each skein of floss usually makes three tassels)

240 6/0 pearlized white seed beads (depending on your preferred length of necklace)

75cm (29½ inches) beading wire

25 silver coloured 6mm jump rings

2 silver coloured calottes (bead tips)

4 silver coloured 2mm crimp beads

Silver coloured toggle clasp

Tools:

Scissors

Four-prong fork

Chain-nose pliers

Round-nose pliers

Wire cutters

Instructions:

1 Cut two lengths of thread: one 10cm (4in) long, one 20cm (7¾in) long. Set aside.

2 Wrap the thread firmly but not too tightly fifteen times around all four prongs of a fork – hold the fork horizontally to do so. Start with one end of the thread extending 1cm (½in) below the lowest prong of the fork and wrap six or seven times, then wrap back over the first layer of wraps. Finish with the tail of the last wrap extending 1cm (½in) below the lowest prong of the fork.

3 Slip the 10cm (4in) length of thread (from step 1) under the wraps at one side of the fork and slide it up and under the fold at the top of the upper prong of the fork. Tie a tight reef knot (square knot). This is the 'hanger thread'.

4 Slide the wraps of thread from the fork. Hold the tassel approximately 0.5cm (¼in) from the knot in the fold (from step 3). Take the 20cm (7in) length of thread (from step 1). With 1–2cm (½–¾in) hanging below the cut end of the tassel, run the thread up to where the tassel is being held – 0.5cm(¼in) from the knot at the top of the tassel. Wrap the thread around the tassel three or four times, creating a head. Tie a tight reef knot and pull down the tails of the knot.

5 Cut the folded threads at the bottom of the tassel (the opposite end of the tassel head) to form the fringe. Trim the tails of the knotted tie from step 4 and the fringe, to create your desired length of tassel.

6 With chain-nose pliers, open a jump ring and slip through the head of the tassel, following the same channel as the 'hanger thread'. Close the jump ring, and remove the hanger thread and knot by carefully cutting off the knot.

7 Thread a crimp bead onto one end of the beading thread. With chain-nose pliers, flatten the crimp bead approximately 0.5cm (¼in) from the end. Repeat with a second crimp bead directly above the first. Trim away any excess wire extending above the second crimp bead.

8 Thread the end of the beading wire (opposite the flattened crimps), passing from the inside to the outside of the calotte cup. Pull the crimps down into the cup and with chain-nose pliers, gently close the two sides of the calotte over the crimps. With round-nose pliers, close the hook of the calotte to form a loop.

9 Thread the beading wire through ten pearlized seed beads. Add a mini tassel followed by ten pearlized seed beads. Continue threading on mini tassels between ten pearlized seed beads until you reach the other end of the necklace. Finish with a final ten beads. The colour sequence for the tassels in our example opposite is: pale pink; fuchsia; purple; white; teal; aqua; pale green; white, repeated.

10 Thread the beading wire through a calotte and a crimp bead. This time, thread the wire from the outside to the inside of the cup. With chain-nose pliers, push the crimp bead down into the cup of the calotte, while pushing together the beads below. Flatten the crimp bead so the beads are close but not not so close that the necklace is stiff. Repeat with a second crimp bead. Trim excess wire. With chain-nose pliers, close the two sides of the calotte over the crimps. With round-nose pliers, close the hook of the calotte to form a loop.

11 With chain-nose pliers, open a jump ring and attach one side of the clasp to the calotte loop at one end of the necklace. Repeat by attaching the other side of the clasp with the remaining jump ring to the other end of the necklace.

Use ring-size memory wire and mini tassels to create wine glass charms.

Polynesia bracelet

Materials:

(for a bracelet of approximately 19–20cm (7½–8in) in length)

1 skein of ivory embroidery floss

40+ 5mm round coral beads

45+ 4mm round turquoise beads

65+ 6/0 Ceylon pearl seed beads

1m (3ft) silver colour beading wire

2 2mm silver colour crimp beads

2 silver colour bead caps (8 x 8mm)

5 6mm (¼in) silver colour jump ring

1 8mm silver colour jump ring

1 12mm lobster (trigger) clasp

Tools:

Four-prong fork

Scissors

Two pairs of chain-nose pliers

Sticky tape or bead stopper

Instructions:

1 Cut two lengths of thread, one 10cm (4in) long and one 20cm (7¾in) long. Set aside.

2 Wrap thread firmly but not to tightly fifteen times around all four prongs of a fork – hold the fork horizontally to do so. Start with one end of the thread extending 1cm (½in) below the lowest prong of the fork. Finish with the tail of the last wrap extending 1cm (½in) below the lowest prong of the fork.

3 Slip the 10cm (4in) length of thread (from step 1) under the wraps at one side of the fork and slide it up and under the fold at the top of the upper prong of the fork. Tie a tight reef knot (square knot). This is the 'hanger thread'.

4 Slide the wraps of thread from the fork. Hold the tassel approximately 0.5cm (¼in) from the knot in the fold (from step 3). Take the 20cm (7¾in) length of thread (from step 1). With 1–2cm (½–¾in) hanging below the cut end of the tassel, run the thread up to where the tassel is being held – 0.5cm (¼in) from the knot at the top of the tassel. Wrap the thread around the tassel three or four times, creating a head. Tie a tight reef knot and pull down the tails of the knot.

5 Cut the folded threads at the bottom of the tassel (the opposite end of the tassel head) to form the fringe. Trim the tails of the knotted tie from step 4, and the fringe, to create your desired length of tassel.

6 With chain-nose pliers, open a jump ring and slip through the head of the tassel, following the same channel as the 'hanger thread'. Close the jump ring. Remove the hanger thread and knot by carefully cutting off the knot.

7 Make a second mini tassel following steps 1–6.

8 With chain-nose pliers, attach a 6mm (¼in) jump ring to the lobster clasp. Set aside.

9 Cut the beading wire into three equal lengths. Pass the three strands through a crimp bead, then around a 6mm (¼in) jump ring and back through the crimp bead until there is a 2–3mm tail. With chain-nose pliers flatten the crimp bead to hold the beading wire tightly around the jump ring, away from the join in the jump ring.

10 Pass the three strands of beading wire through a pearl seed bead and a bead cap (from the outside to the inside of the cap).

11 Thread a strand of coral beads, one strand of turquoise beads and one strand of pearl seed beads to the desired length, leaving at least 4cm (1½in) of wire unthreaded. Use sticky tape (or bead stopper) to keep the beads on the wire.

12 Gently twist the three strands of beads, remove the tape and pass the wire through the bead cap, this time from the inside to the outside. Pass the wire on through a pearl seed bead and a crimp bead.

13 Pass the three strands of beading wire around the 6mm jump ring attached to the lobster clasp from step 8 and back through the crimp bead from step 12. Continue to pass the beading wire strands back through the pearl seed bead and bead cap. Pull the beading wire tight, removing any gaps of wire, then flatten the crimp bead with chain-nose pliers. Trim excess wire.

14 Attach the mini tassels to the small jump ring at the other end of the bracelet. To stagger the tassels, attach one tassel directly to the small jump ring while attaching the second tassel, using a chain of two jump rings.

15 Finally, attach the large jump ring to the same small jump ring as the mini tassels.

Why not create elaborate matching earrings?

Stately table runner

Materials:

13m (42½ft) variegated 3-ply wool

17¾ x 17¾cm (7 x 7in) stiff
  cardboard square

1m (3ft) gold coloured seven-strand
  beading wire

4 5mm gold coloured disc beads

2 8mm round amber glass beads

2 4mm round gold coloured metal beads

2 4cm (1½in) yellow stone heart beads

6 gold coloured 2mm crimp beads

2m (6½ft) sewing thread

Tools:

Scissors

Needle

Chain-nose pliers

Round-nose pliers

Instructions:

1 Cut the wool into two 2m (6½ft) lengths and two 1m (3ft) lengths.

2 Take one 2m (6½ft) length of wool and wrap it firmly but not too tightly, twenty-eight times around the cardboard square. Start with one end of the thread extending 2cm (¾in) below the cardboard. After making twenty-eight wraps, finish with the end of the final wrap extending 2cm (¾in) below the cardboard. Set the excess wool aside.

3 Slip the beading wire under the wraps at one side of the card and slide it up and under the fold at the end away from the cut ends of threads. Bring the two ends together and tie a tight reef knot (square knot). Thread both ends of the wire through a crimp bead and push on top of or as close to the knot as possible and flatten.

4 Slide the wraps of thread from the cardboard. Hold the tassel with the non-dominant hand between thumb and forefinger approximately 3–4cm (1¼–1½in) from the beading wire knot in the fold (from step 3). Take a 1m (3ft) length of wool (from step 1) and follow the instructions for a hidden wrap on page 7.

5 Cut the folds at the bottom of the tassel, at the opposite end of the tassel head. Trim the tassel strands if necessary.

6 Thread both strands of the beading wire through the following: gold disc; amber bead; gold disc; crimp bead; heart bead; gold metal bead and gold crimp bead.

7 Continue by passing the two strands of beading wire around one barrel of a pair of round-nose pliers to create a small round loop, and back through the last crimp bead, gold metal bead, heart bead, gold disc, amber bead and gold disc. Pull the wire taut and with chain-nose pliers flatten the two crimp beads. Cut away excess wire.

8 Make a second wool tassel with remaining length of wool.

9 Finally, use needle and thread to stitch the loop formed in step 7 to the back of a table runner. The table runner shown on the opposite page is 45.5 x 135cm (18 x 53in) when fully laid out.

Use the same technique to make large tassels for a scatter cushion.

Gold Rush necklace

Materials:

5m (16¼ft) fine antique gold coloured chain

3m (9¾ft) fine bright gold coloured chain

Large – 2cm (¾in) – antique gold colour bead cap

15cm (6in) 0.8mm gold coloured craft wire

1 10mm diamante gold coloured bead

1 6mm jet glass bicone bead

10mm gold coloured jump ring

15–17 0.5cm (¼in) antiqued gold coloured jump rings

1 12mm antiqued gold coloured jump ring

Tools:

Chain-nose pliers

Round-nose pliers

Wire cutters

Instructions:

1 Cut eighteen 9cm (3½in) lengths of bright gold chain. Cut thirty-four lengths of antique gold chain.

2 Mix and thread the two tones of gold chain cut in step 1 onto the craft wire. Bring the ends of the wire together so that strands of chain fall into the centre fold. Twist the wire together twice – this will form a circle. Take one tail of wire and wrap it once around the wire at the opposite side of the circle of wire, between strands of chain. Bring the two tails of wire back together and loosely twist together.

3 Pass both wires through the bead cap, the diamante bead and the bicone bead. Use round-nose pliers to make a wrapped loop (see page 7) using the twisted wire.

4 With chain-nose pliers, open the large gold jump ring and close it around the loop formed in step 3, at the top of the bicone bead.

5 With wire cutters, trim the ends of the chain below the bead cap so they are all approximately the same length. As the tassel settles, you may wish to trim some more.

6 Cut two 55cm (21¾in) lengths of bright gold chain and three 55cm (21¾in) lengths of antique gold chain.

7 With chain-nose pliers, open and thread onto a small antique gold jump ring the 55cm (21¾in) lengths of chain from step 6. Attach a second small antique jump ring to the other end of the five lengths of chain.

8 Pass the necklace of 55cm (21¾in) lengths of chain through the large jump ring of the tassel.

9 Attach the lobster clasp to one end of the necklace with a second small jump ring.

10 If you wish to extend the length of your necklace, make a chain of twelve to fifteen small jump rings and attach to the necklace on the side opposite the lobster clasp.

Decorate an antique perfume bottle with a tiny metallic tassel charm.

Volcanic Flame earrings

Materials:

1 skein each of red and black embroidery floss

0.6mm silver colour craft wire

7 x 7cm (2¾ x 2¾in) cardboard square

2 6mm silver colour jump rings

1 pair 6mm silver colour flat pad earring posts

Clear drying adhesive (E6000) or (optional) hot glue gun

Tools:

Scissors

Four-prong fork

Chain-nose pliers

Round-nose pliers

Wire cutters

Instructions:

1 Cut two lengths of red thread, one 10cm (4in) long and one 20cm (7¾in) long. Set aside.

2 Wrap thread firmly but not too tightly thirty times around a 7cm (2¾in) cardboard square. Start with one end of the thread extending 2cm (¾in) below the cardboard. Cut with the end of the final wrap 2cm (¾in) below the cardboard.

3 Slip the 10cm (4in) length of thread (from step 1) under the wraps at one side of the card and slide it up and under the fold at the end away from the cut ends of threads. Tie a tight reef knot (square knot).

4 Slide the wraps of thread from the cardboard. Hold the tassel with your non-dominant hand between thumb and forefinger approximately 1cm (½in) from the knot in the fold (from step 3). Take the 20cm (7¾in) length of thread (from step 1). With 2cm (¾in) hanging below the cut end of the tassel, run the thread up to where the tassel is being held. Wrap the thread around the tassel two or three times, creating a head. Tie a tight reef knot and pull the tails down to the bottom end of the tassel.

5 Cut the folded threads at the bottom of the tassel (the opposite end of the tassel head) to form the fringe. Trim the tails of the knotted tie from step 4 and the fringe, to create the desired length of the tassel.

6 With chain-nose pliers, open a jump ring and slip through the head of the tassel, following the same channel as the 'hanger thread'. Close the jump ring. Remove the hanger thread and knot by carefully cutting off the knot.

7 Cut a 15cm (6in) length of wire. Set aside.

8 Wrap the skein of black thread firmly but not too tightly fifty times around all four prongs of the fork, to form the pompom – hold the fork horizontally to do so. Start with one end of the thread extending 1cm (½in) below the lowest prong of the fork and wrap nine or ten times, then wrap back over the first layer of wraps and continue back and forth until you have fifty wraps. Finish with the tail of the last wrap extending 1cm (½in) below the lowest prong of the fork.

9 Wrap the length of wire two or three times around all the strands of threads between the second and third prongs of the fork. Pull tight and twist two wires together for about 2cm (¾in). Slip the threads off the fork.

10 With round-nose pliers form a wrapped loop (see page 7).

11 Cut all the folds of the pompom. Fluff out and squash the two sides around the wire. Trim the threads to make a round fluffy pompom. Put a little glue around the wire and squash the pompom around the wire to hold the shape and hide the wire. Hold until dry.

12 Attach the jump ring of the tassel to the wire loop of the pompom.

13 Finally, glue the earring post to the centre back of the pompom. A hot glue gun makes this quick and easy. Repeat the steps to make a second earring.

Make your tassels as long, or short, as you like!

Flamingo Fun earrings

Materials:

1 skein each of fuchsia and black twisted craft floss

0.8mm silver colour craft wire

6 x 6cm (2¼ x 2¼in) cardboard square

2 antique silver colour bead caps

2 6mm black glass bicone bead

2 silver coloured earring wires

Tools:

Scissors

Round-nose pliers

Chain-nose pliers

Wire cutters

Instructions:

1 Cut a 10cm (4in) length of craft wire. Set aside.

2 Wrap pink thread firmly but not too tightly fifteen times around the cardboard square. Start with one end of the thread extending 2cm (¾in) below the cardboard. After fifteen wraps, end with the final wrap extending 2cm (¾in) below the cardboard.

3 Repeat step 2 with the black thread next to the fuchsia thread.

4 Slip the wire (from step 1) under all the wraps of both colours, at one side of the card and slide it up and under the fold at the end away from the cut ends of threads. Position the wire so there is 3–4cm (1¼–1½in) on one side of the threads and 6–7cm (2¼–2¾in) on the other side.

5 Fold the short and the long wire ends up so that the threads fall into a 1cm (½in) fold of the wire. Keeping the two colours of thread separated, cross the wires and gently slip from the cardboard.

6 Wrap the shorter wire two or three times around the longer wire close to the coloured threads. Cut away the excess of the shorter wire.

7 Pass the remaining longer wire through the bead cap and the bicone bead. Form a wrapped loop (see page 7).

8 Finally, to complete the earring, open the loop at the bottom of the ear wire with chain-nose pliers and slip on the tassel. Close the loop.

9 Repeat steps 1–8 to make the second earring.

Two-tone tassels make stylish adornments for a wedding-ring cushion and other accessories.

Looped necklace

Materials:

640+ turquoise seed beads

217 jet 3 x 2mm glass rondelles

68 jet 4 x 3mm glass rondelles

1 jet 6 x 4mm glass rondelle

2 silver coloured calottes (bead tips)

2 silver coloured 2mm crimp beads

3m (9¾in) black WildFire thermally
bonded thread

10 x 8mm silver bead caps

18mm silver coloured metal square

3 silver coloured 6mm jump rings

1 silver coloured toggle clasp

10cm (4in) silver coloured
    0.8mm wire

Tools:

Scissors

Chain-nose pliers

Round-nose pliers

Split-eye needle

Sticky tape or bead stopper

Instructions:

1 Make a wrapped loop at one end of the wire (see page 7). Set aside.

2 Cut a 20cm (7¾in) length of WildFire and thread about 1cm (½in) through the split-eye needle. Fold sticky tape over the long end of the thread to prevent beads from coming off. Thread a sequence of ten seed beads and a 3 x 2mm rondelle, seven times. Finish with ten seed beads. Remove the sticky tape. Pass both ends of the thread through a crimp bead, then around the loop of wire from step 1, then back through the crimp bead. Pull the thread ends tight and flatten the crimp bead. Trim excess thread. Repeat this step to make two more bead loops, to be attached to the wrapped loop.

3 Cut another 20cm (7¾in) length of WildFire and thread about 1cm (½in) through the split-eye needle. Fold a piece of sticky tape over the end to prevent beads from coming off. Thread fifteen seed beads and a 3 x 2mm rondelle. Next thread on five sequences of ten seed beads followed by a 3 x 2mm rondelle. Finish with fifteen seed beads. Remove the sticky tape. Pass both ends of the thread through a crimp bead, then around the same loop of wire as the seed beads in step 2, then back through the crimp bead. Pull thread ends tight and flatten the crimp bead. Trim excess thread. Repeat once more.

4 Take a second strand of Wildire and pass 1cm (½in) through the split-eye needle. Thread enough seed beads to equal the length of the strand beads made in step 3. Remember to pass through the same jump ring of the tassel unit, at the halfway point. Remove the needle and fold a piece of sticky tape over the end of the strand of thread to keep beads from coming off while working on the remaining two strands.

5 Take the third strand of WildFire and pass 1cm (½in) through the split-eye needle. Thread enough 3 x 2mm rondelles to equal the length of the strand beads made in steps 3 and 4. Remember to pass through the same jump ring of the tassel unit, at the halfway point.

6 Take three 60cm (23½in) strands of WildFire and pass all three strands through a crimp bead. With chain-nose pliers flatten the crimp bead about 5cm (2in) from one cut end. Tie a knot with the short strands above the flattened crimp bead by taking two strands in one hand and one strand in the other hand and tie a reef knot (square knot). Pull tight and trim excess thread.

7 Thread the other ends of the three strands of WildFire through the calotte, going from the inside of the calotte cup to the outside. Pull the crimps down into the cup of the calotte and with chain-nose pliers, gently close the two sides of the calotte over the crimp and knot. With round-nose pliers, close the hook of the calotte to form a loop.

8 Take one strand of WildFire and pass 1cm (½in) through the split-eye needle. Thread a sequence of two 4 x 3mm rondelles and five seed beads – do this seventeen times. Then pass through the jump ring on the silver square with the tassel and repeat the seed bead and rondelle sequence sixteen more times. Finish with two 4 x 3mm rondelle beads. Remove the needle and fold sticky tape over the end of the strand of thread to keep the beads from coming off while working on the remaining two strands.

9 Take a second strand of Wildire and pass 1cm (½in) through the split-eye needle. Thread enough seed beads to equal the length of the strand beads made in step 8. Remember to pass through the same jump ring of the tassel unit, at the halfway point. Remove the needle and fold sticky tape over the end of the strand of thread to keep beads from coming off.

10 Take the third strand of WildFire and pass 1cm (½in) through the split-eye needle. Thread enough 3 x 2mm rondelles to equal the length of the strand beads made in steps 8 and 9. Pass through the same jump ring of the tassel unit.

11 Remove the needle from the third strand. Remove the sticky tape from strands 1 and 2 and thread all three through a calotte and a crimp bead, from the outside

of the calotte to the inside of the cup. With chain-nose pliers, push the crimp bead down deep into the cup of the calotte, while pushing together the beads below. Flatten the crimp bead so the beads are close together but not so close that the necklace is stiff. Tie a reef knot above the flattened crimp bead – take two strands in one hand and one strand in the other. Pull the ends tight and trim excess thread. With chain-nose pliers, gently close the two sides of the calotte over the crimp and knot. With round-nose pliers, close the hook of the calotte to form a loop.

12 With chain-nose pliers, open a jump ring and attach one side of the clasp to the calotte loop at one end of the necklace. Repeat by attaching the other side of the clasp with the remaining jump ring to the other end of the necklace.

Loops of crystals threaded through decorative buttons make sophisticated earrings

Feathered necklace

Materials:

Feathers of choice, about 10cm (4in) long: can be cut down to the appropriate size depending on size of bead cone

1.35m (4¼ft) fine silver coloured chain

2 bead cones

2 3mm silver coloured beads

2 silver coloured 6mm jump rings

0.8mm silver coloured wire

Tools:

Wire cutters

Chain-nose pliers

Instructions:

1 Cut a 20cm (7¾in) piece of wire. Fold in half.

2 If necessary, cut down your feathers to the length that looks best with your choice of bead cone (remembering the extra length of the bead cone). In your non-dominant hand, arrange the feathers in a bunch and place them in the fold of the wire from step 1.

3 Wrap one of the wire halves around the feathers, about 1cm (½in) from the feather tips.

4 Thread the wires and feather bunch through a bead cone and a small silver coloured bead, and, following the instructions on page 7, form a wrapped loop.

5 With chain-nose pliers, open a jump ring and attach the feather tassel to one end of the chain.

6 Make a second feather tassel to attach to the other end of the chain.

A feather tassel makes a perfect bookmark.

Candyfloss bag charm

Materials:

A collection of threads, fancy wool, and ribbons

0.8mm silver coloured craft wire

Decorative bead cap

5 6mm (¼in) silver coloured jump rings

15mm silver coloured lobster (trigger) clasp

18cm (7in) silver coloured chain

Choice of silver coloured charms

Tools:

Scissors

Wire cutter

Round-nose pliers

Chain-nose pliers

Instructions:

1 Cut a 10cm (4in) length of wire. Fold in half and set aside.

2 From your choice of mixed threads, fancy wool and ribbons, cut multiple strands approximately 12cm (4¾in) long (we have eight strands each of eight different threads, fancy wool and ribbons). Mix them up and bunch them so they are layered side by side. The layered bunch should extend to a total width of 2–3cm (¾–1¼in).

3 Slip the fold of the wire from step 1 around the centre of the threads, wool and ribbons from step 2. Wrap one half of the wire (call this wire A) around all the strands of ribbon and threads, two or three times, and pull tight. With the remaining wire (call this wire B), make two or three wraps around wire A, close to the ribbon and threads. Trim any excess from wire B.

4 Fold the strands of threads, wool and ribbons together and down with wire A at the top. Pass wire through the bead cap and form a wrapped loop (see page 7). Take this opportunity to trim the tassel ends if necessary.

5 Attach each charm to the chain with a jump ring.

6 Attach the tassel and the chain of charms to the lobster clasp using a jump ring.

A tasselled necklace made in the same fashion as the bag charm makes the ideal festival accessory.

Deck the Halls pendant

Materials:

Door knob (with a hole running from front to back)

Red twisted embroidery floss

Gold metallic embroidery thread

10 x 10cm (4 x 4in) cardboard square

3 12 x 6mm decorative bead caps – antique gold with crystal diamantes

2 7mm round diamante bead

2 10 x 9 faceted crystal rondelle beads

0.8 gold colour craft wire

10mm (½in) gold colour jump ring

Gold coloured fine fancy chain

Red 6mm grosgrain ribbon, 36cm (14in) length

Tools:

Scissors

Wire cutters

Chain-nose pliers

Round-nose pliers

Instructions:

1 Cut a 25cm (9¾in) piece of gold coloured wire. Set aside.

2 Wrap red floss firmly but not too tightly around the cardboard square. Start with one end of the red floss extending 1–2cm (½–¾in) below the cardboard and make thirty wraps with the end of the final wrap extending 1–2cm (½–¾in) below the cardboard. In the same way, make twenty-two wraps with the gold thread, over the red floss.

3 Slip the wire (from step 1) under the wraps at one side of the card and slide it up and under the fold at the end away from the cut ends of threads. Fold the wire in half and twist to hold threads in place.

4 Slide the wraps of thread from the cardboard.

5 Cut the folds at the bottom of the tassel, at the opposite end of the wire.

6 Thread both ends of wire through the following sequence: bead cap (from inside to outside of cap); diamante bead; bead cap (from outside to inside); 10 x 9 faceted crystal rondelle beads; doorknob; 10 x 9 faceted crystal rondelle beads; bead cap (from inside to outside); diamante bead.

7 Form a wrapped loop above the last bead (see page 7).

8 Use chain-nose pliers to open the jump ring and thread through the links at each end of the chain and then the doorknob tassel. Close the jump ring.

9 Tie a ribbon bow just below the jump ring.

Upcycle crystal doorknobs to make unusual heirloom decorations in a variety of colour schemes.

Wild West key fob

Materials:

1.5m (5ft) of each of three colours of 3mm wide flat leather suede

75cm (30in) tan coloured thin leather cord

0.6mm silver craft wire

Key fob (the fob pictured opposite is 4.5cm/1¾in wide)

Clear drying adhesive (E6000)

Tools:

Scissors

Instructions:

1 Cut a 25cm (9¾in) strand of leather cord. Set aside.

2 Cut five or six 15cm (6in) strands of flat suede. Set aside the remaining flat suede of the same colour.

3 Layer the suede strands side by side in two layers. Take the remaining suede of the same colour and slip under the centre of the layers of suede strands to the centre of long strand of suede. Tie a knot to hold the multiple strands together.

4 Fold down the multiple strands of suede and hold in one hand. Take the leather cord from step 1 and following the instructions on page 7, make a hidden wrap three or four times to form a head to the tassel, about 0.5cm (¼in) from the knot. Trim away excess leather cord.

5 Trim the strands at the bottom of the tassel.

6 Repeat with the other two colours of suede.

7 Cut three pieces of wire, each 10cm (4in) long. Cut two 10cm (4in) lengths of leather suede. Set aside.

8 Arrange the three tassels, staggered and side-by-side.

9 Working with one tassel at a time, pass the two strands of suede at the top of each tassel around the key fob. Take a length of wire from step 7 and wrap two or three times around the resulting four strands of suede, directly below the key fob, twist and cut excess wire. Repeat with the remaining two tassels.

10 Glue the two strands of suede from step 7 to hide the wire holding the tassels to the key fob. Trim the suede so that they meet together.

11 Finally, trim the suede ends below the covered wire so they are neat and even.

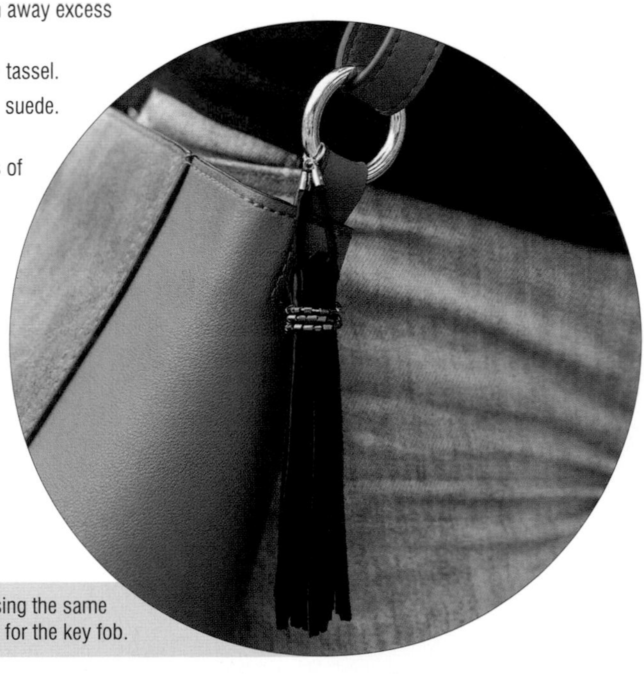

Craft a suede leather bag charm using the same techniques as for the key fob.

Dinner Date necklace

Materials:

2 skeins black embroidery floss

6 x 6cm (2¼ x 2¼in) cardboard square

100 jet 6 x 4 faceted glass rondelles

18 gold colour 6mm diamante rondelle spacers

10 aurora borealis 6mm bicone beads

2 gold colour 3mm metal beads

1 fancy antiqued gold 15mm bead cap

10cm (4in) gold colour 0.8mm wire

60cm (24in) gold beading wire

1 gold colour crimp beads

3 gold colour 4mm jump rings

1 gold colour 7mm jump ring

1 gold colour 12mm lobster clasp

Tools:

Scissors

Chain-nose pliers

Round-nose pliers

Instructions:

1 Wrap a skein of black embroidery floss firmly but not too tightly fifty times around the cardboard square. Start with one end of the thread extending 1cm (½in) below the cardboard and with the end of the final wrap extending 1cm (½in) below the cardboard.

2 Slip the wire under the wraps at one side of the card with 3cm (1¼in) on one side and 6cm (2¼in) on the other. Slide it up and under the fold at the end away from the cut ends of threads. Bring the wire ends together with the 6cm (2¼in) piece of wire upwards. Pull the threads together tightly by twisting the shorter end of wire around the base of the longer piece. Trim the shorter wire excess.

3 Slide the wraps of thread from the cardboard. Cut the folds at the bottom of the tassel, at the opposite end of the twisted wire to form the fringe.

4 Thread the remaining wire up through the bead cap and through one rondelle bead. Pull tight and form a wrapped loop (see page 7).

5 Trim the tassel to your preferred length and make sure all strands are even.

6 Thread a crimp bead onto one end of the beading wire. Fold 2cm (¾in) of wire over a 4mm (¼in) jump ring and back through the crimp bead. Use chain-nose pliers to flatten the crimp bead.

7 Thread a gold metal bead followed by five sequences of: ten rondelle beads; diamante rondelle spacer; bicone bead and diamante rondelle spacer.

8 Remove the last diamante rondelle and add the bead cap tassel followed by four sequences of: bicone bead; diamante rondelle spacer; ten rondelle beads and diamante rondelle spacer.

9 Complete the bead sequence with: bicone bead; diamante rondelle spacer; ten rondelle beads; metal bead; crimp bead.

10 Fold the beading wire around a 4mm jump ring and back through the crimp bead and at least two or three beads (gold metal and jet rondelles). Pull the wire until all the gaps are removed but not so tightly that the necklace is stiff. Flatten the crimp bead. Trim away any excess wire.

11 With chain-nose pliers, open a 4mm jump ring and attach the lobster clasp to the jump ring at one end of the necklace. Open the 7mm jump ring and attach to the small jump ring at the other end of the necklace.

Top off your date night ensemble with a pair of matching earrings.

Santa Fe necklace

Materials:

100 6mm (¼in) turquoise beads

100 4mm tiger eye beads

360+ turquoise seed beads

3 6 x 7.5cm (2¼ x 3in) flat suede leather pieces

3 5cm (2in) strands of thin beige leather cord or waxed cotton cord

WildFire (thermally bonded thread) in black or crystal

7 x 2.5mm silver plated washer bead

6mm (¼in) silver coloured jump rings

2mm silver coloured crimp beads

2 2mm silver coloured crimp beads

2 silver coloured calottes (bead tips)

1 silver coloured toggle clasp

Clear drying adhesive (E6000)

Tools:

Heavy-duty scissors

Chain-nose pliers

Round-nose pliers

Split-eye needle

Sticky tape or bead stopper

Instructions:

See page 6 for more direction on making rolled tassels.

1 Mark your 6 x 7.5cm (2¼ x 3in) piece of suede leather about 1cm (½in) from the top. With large, heavy-duty scissors, make twelve to fourteen cuts up to the 1cm (½in) mark. Each cut should be 6–6.5cm (2¼–2½in) long, and about 4–5cm (1½–2in) wide.

2 Lay the fringed piece with the tassel head to the right and the fringe to the left. Take a 5cm (2in) piece of thin leather cord – fold it in half and glue it to the edge of the tassel head with clear drying adhesive. Keep 5–6mm (¼in) of the fold above the edge of the suede. Hold the fold of the cord together until the glue sets enough that the cord loop doesn't spread open, then let dry.

3 Smear the adhesive generously along the middle of the tassel head. Take the edge of the tassel head, where the leather cord loop is attached. Fold the left edge of the tassel head and push down hard before rolling the fringed suede tightly to the end. Hold until dry.

4 Slip the leather cord loop through a silver washer bead. With chain-nose pliers, open a jump ring and pass it through the leather cord loop that extends above the washer bead. Close the jump ring.

5 Pass about 3cm (1¼in) of WildFire through the split-eye needle and string with 100–120 seed beads. Holding the thread end opposite the needle with your non-dominant hand, circle the tassel head with three strands of seed beads. Weave the needle end of the thread back through the beads in the middle and first strand of beads to where the other end of the thread is. Tie a reef knot (square knot) and seal the knot with adhesive. Weave both tails of the knot back through the seed beads and cut any excess thread.

6 Make two more rolled tassels.

7 Cut two 60cm (23½in) lengths of WildFire. Hold the two lengths side by side and tie them together in an overhand knot about 2.5cm (1in) from one end. Pull the knot tight and seal with adhesive.

8 Pass the short ends of the thread through a crimp bead, slipping the crimp bead over the knot. With chain-nose pliers, flatten the crimp bead. Trim away any excess thread.

9 Pass the long ends through the calotte, from the inside to the outside of the cup. Allow the flattened crimp to rest inside the calotte. With chain-nose pliers, gently close the cup of the calotte over the flattened crimp.

10 Thread the split-eye needle with approximately 3cm (1¼in) of one strand of the threads. String on the following sequence of beads: twenty-eight turquoise beads; silver washer; turquoise bead; tassel; turquoise bead; silver washer; ten turquoise beads; silver washer; turquoise bead; tassel; turquoise bead; silver washer; ten turquoise beads; silver washer; turquoise bead; tassel; turquoise bead; silver washer and twenty-eight turquoise beads. Remove the needle and use a piece of sticky tape (or bead stopper) to keep the beads from coming off while you work on the remaining strands.

11 Thread 3cm (1¼in) of the second strand through the needle. String thirty-nine tiger eye beads then pass the thread through the silver washer, turquoise bead, tassel, turquoise bead and silver washer from the first strand of beads (from step 10).

12 String fourteen tiger eye beads then pass through the next group of silver washer, turquoise bead, tassel turquoise bead and silver washer on the bead strand from step 10.

13 Repeat step 12, then complete the second strand with another thirty tiger eye beads.

14 Remove the sticky tape (or bead stopper) from the strand of turquoise beads. Pass both threads through a calotte from the outside to the inside of the cup, then through a crimp bead. With chain-nose pliers push the crimp bead down deep into the cup of the calotte and flatten. Tie a knot above the crimp bead. Seal with clear drying adhesive and trim excess thread.

15 With chain-nose pliers, gently close the cup of the calotte to hide the crimp and knot.

16 With round-nose pliers, close the hook above both calottes to form a closed loop.

17 With chain-nose pliers, open a jump ring and attach one side of the clasp to the loop of the calotte formed in step 16. Repeat with the other side of the clasp and the other end of the necklace to complete.

Strong patterned paper can be folded and cut to make attractive decorative tassels.

La Fiesta bangle

Materials:

1 wooden bangle base – the featured bangle is 8cm (3¼in) in diameter

Thin, tan waxed cotton cord (amount dependent on size of bangle base)

1 60cm (23½in) – depending on size of bangle base – length of 6mm wide fabric strip

26 11–12cm (4¼–4¾in) lengths of 6mm (¼in)-wide fabric strips

6 6mm silver coloured jump rings

Clear drying adhesive (E6000)

Tools:

Scissors

Chain-nose pliers

Instructions:

1 Lay thirteen strips of fabric, right side up, in a bunch together, side by side and layered on top of one another.

2 Cut a 10cm (4in) piece of cord. Pass the cord under and around the centre of the strips of fabric from step 1. Tie a tight reef knot (square knot). Seal the knot with adhesive and allow to dry.

3 Cut a 15cm (6in) piece of cord. Fold the strips of fabric down and hold in the non-dominant hand. Take the 15cm (6in) piece of cord and make a hidden wrap (following the instructions on page 7), about 5mm (¼in) from the knot from step 2. Trim away excess cord.

4 Cut each strip of the fringe in half lengthways for a fuller, fluffier tassel.

5 Slip an open jump ring around the knot, close the jump ring with chain-nose pliers and set aside.

6 Make a second tassel.

7 Cover the wooden bangle with the waxed cotton cord by spreading a thin layer of adhesive over 2–3cm (¾–1¼in) of the bangle at a time, then wrapping the cord around and over the glue. It is easier if you leave the cord on the card or in a ball and pass the whole card around and through the opening of the wood bangle.

8 To finish, cut the cord, leaving a 2cm (¾in) tail. Spread a thin layer of adhesive on the back side of the tail and slip under two or three previous placed strands of cord.

9 Wrap the 60cm (23½in) strip of fabric around the cord covered bangle about 1–1.5cm (½in) apart. Spread a thin layer of adhesive here and there on the wrong side of the fabric. Glue the ends down. Let dry.

10 With chain-nose pliers, open a jump ring and slip it under and around a strand of cord that is covering the wood bangle on one side of a fabric strip. Close the jump ring. Repeat with a second jump ring on the other side of the same fabric strip.

11 Attach one tassel to one of the jump rings placed in step 10 by opening the jump ring already on the tassel. Close the jump ring.

12 To stagger the tassels, attach a second jump ring to the jump ring on the remaining tassel. Take a third jump ring and attach the second jump ring to the remaining jump ring placed in step 10.

Attaching a lobster clasp to a tassel means it can be placed and removed easily.

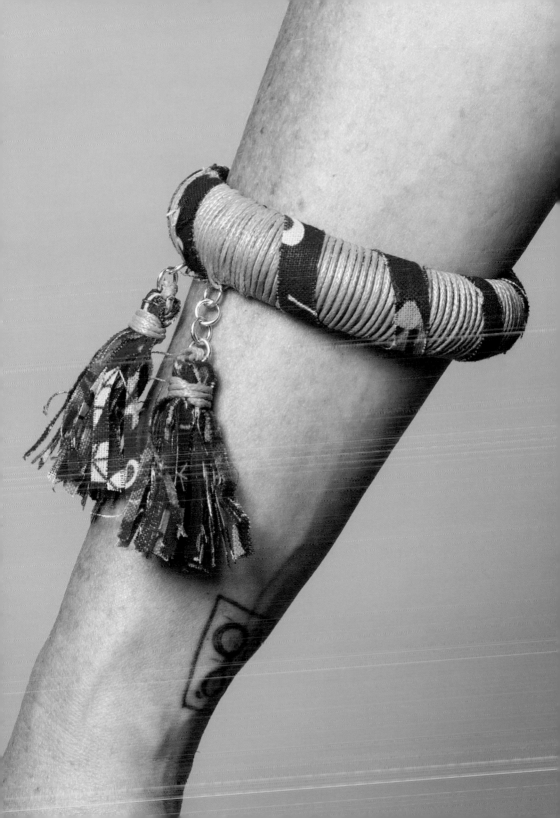

Irish Luck candle wrap

Materials:

0.6mm silver coloured craft wire

0.8mm silver coloured craft wire

1 skein each in two colours of twisted embroidery thread

6 x 6cm (2¼ x 2¼in) cardboard square

Candle, 22.5cm (8¾in) circumference

Tools:

Wire cutters

Round-nose pliers

Chain-nose pliers

Flat-nose pliers

Instructions:

1 Cut 10cm (4in) of 0.8mm wire. Set aside.

2 Wrap thread firmly but not too tightly thirty times around the cardboard square. Start with one end of the thread extending 1cm (½in) below the cardboard. After making the wraps, end with a tail extending 1cm (½in) below the cardboard.

3 Slip the wire (from step 1) under the wraps at one side of the card and slide it up and under the fold at the end away from the cut ends of threads. Wrap one half of the wire (call this wire A) around the other half of the wire (call this wire B). Make two wraps and cut any excess from wire A. Slip the wrapped threads from the cardboard.

4 With wire B, form a wrapped loop (see page 7). The wraps from the wrapped loop made with wire B should meet with the wraps made with wire A in step 3.

5 Hold the tassel with your non-dominant hand, between thumb and forefinger approximately 0.5cm (¼in) from the top of the tassel. Take a 40cm (15¾in) length of 0.6mm wire and wrap around the tassel to form a head, organically (i.e. untidily!) – include a decorative loop part-way through, until there is 6–8cm (2¼–3¼in) wire left.

Warning

Ensure your wrap is not positioned too close to the tip of the candle. Exercise extreme caution with the tassels and wire when the candle is alight.

6 With chain-nose and flat-nose pliers, form a flat coil at the end of the wire (see page 7), and use round-nose pliers to make curls with any wire that remains.

7 Take about 4m (13ft) of 0.6mm wire and wrap it twelve times, untidily, around the candle. Thread on one tassel before twisting the tails of the wire to hold the tassel in place.

8 Repeat with a second 4m (13ft) length of 0.6mm wire, this time starting and finishing above the first round of wire, and about 1cm (½in) to the right.

9 Use chain-nose and flat-nose pliers to form different-sized flat coils at the ends of the wire tails (see page 7). Use round-nose pliers to make curls where any straight wire remains.

Wire coils add an attractive detail to a tasselled necklace.

Pretty Pink lampshade

Materials:

Small lampshade – 11.5cm (4½in) diameter at top, 17cm (6¾in) diameter at bottom

Three shades of pink embroidery floss: the amount is dependent on the size of lampshade – each skein makes three to four pompoms

Variegated pink embroidery floss: the amount is dependent on the size of lamp shade – each skein makes three to four pompoms

0.6mm silver colour craft wire

5 x 5cm (2 x 2in) cardboard square

Clear drying adhesive (E6000) or (optional) hot glue gun

Tools:

Scissors

Four-prong fork

Chain-nose pliers

Round-nose pliers

Pencil or tailor's chalk

Instructions:

1 Cut two lengths of thread: one 10cm (4in) long, one 20cm (7¾in) long. Set aside.

2 Wrap the remaining thread firmly but not too tightly, thirty times around the cardboard square. Start with one end of the thread extending 2cm (¾in) below the cardboard. Finish with the end of the final wrap extending 2cm (¾in) below the cardboard.

3 Slip the 10cm (4in) length of thread (from step 1) under the wraps at one side of the card and slide it up and under the fold at the end away from the cut ends of threads. Tie a tight reef knot (square knot).

4 With chain-nose pliers, open a jump ring. Slide the wraps of thread from the cardboard. Hold the tassel and slip the jump ring around the tassel threads held by the knot in step 3. Close the jump ring. Trim the thread tails of the knot, close to the knot.

5 Now hold the tassel approximately 1cm (½in) from the knot in the fold (from step 3). Take the 20cm (7¾in) length of thread (from step 1). With 2cm (¾in) hanging below the cut end of the tassel, run the thread up to where the tassel is being held. Wrap the thread around the tassel two or three times, creating a head. Tie a tight reef knot and pull down the tails to the cut end of the tassel.

6 Cut the folds of threads at the bottom of the tassel at the opposite end of the tassel head to form the fringe. Trim the ends of the knotted tie from step 4 and any other thread ends that extend beyond the desired length of the tassel.

7 Make the required number of tassels – the lampshade pictured opposite features fifteen.

8 Cut a 15cm (6in) length of wire. Set aside.

9 To make the pompom, wrap thread firmly but not too tightly fifty times around all four prongs of the fork. Start with one end of the thread extending 1cm (½in) below the lowest prong of the fork and wrap nine or ten times, then wrap back over the first layer of wraps and continue back and forth until you have fifty wraps. Finish with the tail of the last wrap extending 1cm (½in) below the lowest prong of the fork.

10 Wrap the length of wire two or three times around all strands of thread, between the central two prongs of the fork. Pull tight and twist together two wires for about 2cm (¾in). With round-nose pliers form a wrapped loop (see page 7) and trim any excess wire.

Note: A pompom with a wire loop is for those pompoms which will have a tassel attached to it. For those pompoms without a tassel, no loop needs to be formed – just trim off any excess wire.

11 Cut all the folds of the pompom. Fluff out and squash the two sides around the wire. Trim the threads to make a round fluffy pompom. Put a little glue around the wire and squash the pompom around the wire until dry. This will hold the pompom shape and hide the wire.

12 Make pompoms with wire loops from variegated thread. Attach a tassel to each pompom. Use three shades of pink tassels to reflect the colours in the variegated pompoms.

13 Make pompoms without wire loops for the top of the lampshade and for placing between the pompoms with tassels, using the palest shade of pink floss.

14 Attach the pompoms to the lampshade – the easiest and fastest way is to use a hot glue gun. Clear drying adhesive can be used but you will need to hold pompoms in place until set.

Top of the lampshade: Place the plain pompoms next to one another around the top edge.

Bottom of the lampshade: Measure and mark the position of the pompoms with tassels, using a pencil or tailor's chalk. We have marked the bottom of our lampshade every 4cm (1½in). Glue the pompoms with tassels first, then fill the spaces between these with pompoms without tassels.

Create a unique bag charm that also combines tassels with brightly coloured pompoms.

Rustic Chic lampshade

Materials:

Lampshade – 18cm (7in) diameter at top, 23cm (9in) diameter at bottom

Jute or hemp cord

6.5 x 6.5cm (2½ x 2½in) cardboard square

Wooden hearts – 2 x 1cm (¾ x ½in) – in two different tones or colours (there are 43 hearts altogether on this lampshade)

Clear drying adhesive (E6000) or (optional) hot glue gun

Tools:

Scissors

Pencil or tailor's chalk

Instructions:

1 Cut three lengths of cord, each 20cm (7¾in) long. Set aside.

2 Wrap the jute firmly but not too tightly, fifteen times around the cardboard square. Start with one end of the thread extending 2cm (¾in) below the cardboard. Finish with the final wrap extending 2cm (¾in) below the cardboard.

3 Slip two lengths of jute (from step 1) under the wraps at one side of the card and slide them up and under the fold at the end away from the cut ends of threads. Tie a tight reef knot (square knot).

4 Slide the wraps of thread from the cardboard. Hold the tassel with your non-dominant hand between thumb and forefinger approximately 1cm (½in) from the knot of the bow (from step 3). Take the remaining length of jute (from step 1). With 1cm (½in) hanging below the cut end of the tassel, run the thread up to where the tassel is being held. Wrap the thread around the tassel two or three times, creating a head. Tie a tight reef knot (square knot). Pull down the tails as far as the cut end of the tassel.

5 Cut the folds at the bottom of the tassel, at the opposite end of the tassel head.

6 Trim the ends of the knotted tie from step 4 and any other thread ends that extend beyond the desired length of the tassel. Tie a bow with the tails of the knot from step 3. Make fourteen of these for a lampshade of this size.

7 Mark the bottom edge of the lampshade in pencil or chalk with the positioning of the tassels. This may vary with different sizes of lampshades. We have marked our lampshade every 5cm (2in).

8 Glue the knot (below the bow of the tassel) just above the bottom edge of the lampshade over the markings from the previous step.

9 Glue small wooden hearts just below the bow on each tassel, then more along the top edge of the lampshade. If you have two different coloured hearts, you can alternate the colours around the lampshade.

Bows complement tassels perfectly for a neat finish.

Flamenco Fan earrings

Materials:

Twisted embroidery floss in two or three colours

2 8mm silver coloured bead caps

2 6mm silver coloured diamante rondelles

2 6mm orchid coloured glass bicone beads

0.8mm silver coloured craft wire

2 silver coloured ear wires

Clear nail varnish or clear drying adhesive (E6000)

Tools:

Scissors

Four-prong fork

Wire cutters

Chain-nose pliers

Round-nose pliers

Sewing needle

Instructions:

1 Cut two lengths of thread, one 10cm (4in) long and one 20cm (8in) long. Set aside.

2 Wrap the remaining thread firmly but not too tightly thirty times around all four prongs of a fork – hold the fork horizontally to do so. Start with one end of the thread extending 1cm (½in) below the lowest prong of the fork. Wrap back and forth in layers. Finish with the tail of the last wrap extending 1cm (½in) below the lowest prong of the fork.

3 Slip the 10cm (4in) length of thread (from step 1) under the wraps at one side of the fork and slide it up and under the fold at the top of the upper prong of the fork. Tie a tight reef knot (square knot). This is the 'hanger thread'.

4 Slide the wraps of thread from the fork. Hold the tassel with the non-dominant hand between thumb and forefinger approximately 0.5cm (¼in) from the knot in the fold (from step 3). Take the 20cm (8in) length of thread (from step 1). With 10cm (4in) hanging below the cut end of the tassel, run the thread up to where the tassel is being held – 0.5cm (¼in) from the knot at the top of the tassel. Wrap the thread around the tassel two or three times, creating a head. Tie a tight reef knot and pull down the tails.

5 Cut the folds of threads at the bottom of the tassel, at the opposite end of the tassel head. Trim the ends of the knotted tie from step 4 and any other thread ends that extend beyond the desired length of the tassel.

6 Seal the knot above the tassel head with clear drying adhesive or clear nail varnish. When dry, trim tails close to the knot.

7 Repeat steps 1–6 to make two more tassels.

8 Take a 30cm (11¾in) length of twisted floss and unwind the strands that make up the twisted floss. Thread needle with a single strand. Knot the long end. Sew the three mini tassels together. Start by turning the bottom tassel upside down and spread the threads apart to expose the centre. Pass the needle through the centre and up through the head of the tassel, missing the knot.

9 Turn the second or middle tassel upside down, spreading threads apart to open the centre. Now pass the needle through the centre of the second tassel, up through the head of the tassel, missing the knot. Pull the first (bottom) tassel up to rest at the centre of the second (middle) tassel. Let the strands of thread of the second (middle) tassel fall down and around the first (bottom) tassel. Repeat with the third tassel and tie off thread.

10 With two or three more strands of thread, repeat steps 8 and 9 to secure.

11 Take a 6cm (2¼in) piece of wire and pass 2cm (¾in) under the knot of the top (last) tassel. Fold both ends of wire up and together. Take the 2cm (¾in) wire end and make two or three tight wraps around the 6cm (2¼in), close to the fold. Cut away excess wire.

12 Pass the remaining wire up through the bead cap, then continue through a diamante rondelle and a bicone bead. Make a wrapped loop (see page 7).

13 With chain-nose pliers, open the loop at the bottom of the ear wire, slip on the tiered tassel and close the loop.

14 Repeat steps 1–13 to make the second earring.

Make a tiered tassel charm
for a jazzy notebook.

Acknowledgements

I would like to thank the team at Search Press for their patience and support, particularly Beth Harwood for editorial support, Stacy Grant for her amazing photography, Juan Hayward for his design work, and Emma Sutcliffe for turning my very messy drawings into clear, helpful diagrams.

A special mention goes to my 'BFF', Vivian Peritts, who helped me to learn very quickly about textiles and the tricks for making tassels.

Of course I must also thank all who have purchased a copy of this book. It truly is my wish that it will inspire you and bring you much pleasure.

Please visit my website at:
www.carolynschulz.com